MANDALA
COLORING BOOK

MANDALA
COLORING BOOK
Beautiful designs to inspire creativity

SIRIUS

SIRIUS

This edition published in 2023 by Sirius Publishing, a division of
Arcturus Publishing Limited,
26/27 Bickels Yard, 151–153 Bermondsey Street,
London SE1 3HA

ISBN: 978-1-3988-2556-7
CH008563NT
Supplier 29, Date 1222, PI 00002981

Printed in China

Created for children 10+

Introduction

The beautiful configurations of geometric symbols that comprise a mandala are used in a number of spiritual traditions. They first appeared in Buddhist art in India in the first century BCE. They may be used to focus the attention, as spiritual guidance tools, as an aid to meditation and the inducing of trances, and to establish a sacred space. Many eastern religions use mandalas to represent deities, or paradises, or actual shrines. Within New Age symbolism, mandalas represent the cosmos in either a metaphysical or spiritual way.

The majority of mandalas in this coloring book do not have special spiritual or ritual significance but have been specially created as designs for coloring. Their repetitive nature is especially calming when you're using coloring as a way to wind down and relax.

Take either colored pencils or felt tip pens and use your own taste and style to decide on a color palette for your mandalas. Some of them may suggest a bright scheme, while others may be more suited to pastel tones. Whatever your preferences, you'll while away hours coloring in these spiritual images.